Science in Early Islamic Culture

كوتيع غيرت

George Beshore

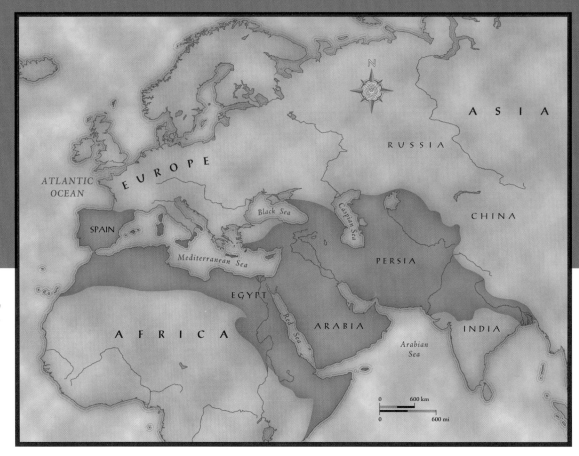

Science in Early Islamic Culture

George Beshore

كوتع غيرت ا

Science of the Past

FRANKLIN WATTS

A Division of Grolier Publishing
New York • London • Hong Kong • Sydney
Danbury, Connecticut

Photographs ©: Ancient Art & Architecture Collection: 24, 10, 12 (Richard Sheridan); Archive Photos: 34 (Giraudon); Art Resource: 21, 50, 25, 57 (Giraudon), 22, 56 (Erich Lessing), 53 (Scala); Bodleian Library: 33, 39; Courtesy of Bausch & Lomb: 44 (Rochester, New York); E.T Archive: cover, 20; Metropolitan Museum of Art: 30; National Library of Medicine: 37, 40, 41, 42; New York Public Library Picture Collection: 45; North Wind Picture Archives: 9, 55; Photo Researchers: 23, 48 (M.Claye/Jacana); Superstock, Inc.: 32, 38, 46, 52, 47 (John W. Warden); The British Museum: 19; UPI/Corbis-Bettmann: 6, 8, 15, 18, 28, 31, 35, 36, 49.

Map created by XNR Productions Inc.

Illustrations by Drew-Brook-Cormack Associates

Library of Congress Cataloging-in-Publication Data

Beshore, George.
Science in early Islamic culture / George Beshore. —Rev. ed.
p. cm. — (Science of the past)
Includes bibliographical references and index.
Summary: Discusses the extraordinary scientific discoveries and advancements in the Islamic world after the birth of Muhammad in 570 and their impact on Western civilization in subsequent centuries and today.
ISBN 0-531-20355-7 (lib. bdg.)   0-531-15917-5 (pbk.)
1. Science—Islamic Empire—History—Juvenile literature.   2. Science, Ancient—Juvenile literature.   3. Islamic Empire—History—622–661—Juvenile literature.   4. Islam—History—Juvenile literature. [1. Science—Islamic Empire—History.   2. Science, Ancient.   3. Islamic Empire—History—622–661.] I. Title. II. Series.
Q127.I74B47   1998
509'.17'6710902—dc21   97-5012
                                                   CIP
                                                   AC

CONTENTS

chapter 1

A New Era in Science

کتنع غیرت ا

و عاشق ی

From around 500 to 1400, Europe was divided into small kingdoms or estates. Most common people were farmers.

About 1,400 years ago, the people living in Europe seemed to have no interest in science or scientific discovery. At that time, most of the world's ancient civilizations lay in ruins. Ancient Egypt, the first great culture to fall, was conquered by Alexander the Great, a Greek ruler, about 2,300 years ago. Over the next 200 years, internal fighting weakened the power of the Greek Empire. Finally, Greece fell to the Romans in 146 B.C.

For hundreds of years after that, the Roman Empire ruled most of Europe as well as parts of Asia and Africa. Eventually, Roman rulers

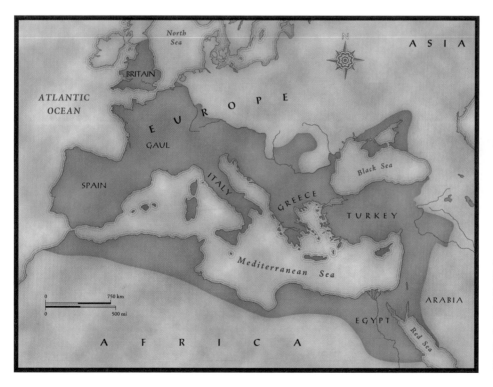

At it's height the Roman Empire included most of Europe and parts of Africa and Asia close to the Mediterranean Sea.

7

began to have trouble maintaining control over their vast territory. As military and political leaders struggled among themselves for power, the Roman Empire grew weaker and weaker. In 476, Germanic barbarians attacked Rome, overthrew the emperor, and divided the Roman Empire into several smaller kingdoms.

The world's great civilizations—Egypt, Greece, and Rome—no longer existed. Europe was now governed by kings and nobles who controlled small kingdoms or estates. These rulers spent their time fighting each other for land and possessions. Most of the common people were poor and uneducated. They spent their time farming. Few people had time to study ancient texts or observe the world around them. As a result, most of the knowledge gained by ancient civilizations was lost.

The Birth of Islam

The ancient Egyptian, Greek, and Roman scientists had made remarkable advances in medicine, math, astronomy, philosophy, and *alchemy.* Their discoveries might have been lost forever if a child named Muhammad had not been born in Arabia around 570.

Around the year 610, Muhammad had a vision that inspired him to develop a new religion, which he called Islam.

Muhammad fleeing
to Medina

When Muhammad was about 40 years old, he had a vision in a cave near the city of Mecca, in what is now Saudi Arabia. Muhammad felt he had been called to be a prophet of God. At that time, most Arabs worshipped nature gods and prayed to idols and spirits. Muhammad believed that it was his mission to develop a new religion that would unite all people under Allah, the one true God. The religion Muhammad founded is called *Islam*.

The Arabs living in Mecca rejected Muhammad's teachings and forced him to flee to the city of Medina. As Muhammad began to preach in the markets of Medina, people rallied around him. They accepted Muhammad as God's messenger and adopted Islam as their religion. Muhammad's followers called themselves *Muslims.*

Like Muhammad, all Muslims wanted to spread Islamic beliefs throughout the world. After Muhammad's death in 632, Muslim leaders decided that they should use military force to convert as many people as possible.

The Muslims formed mighty armies that swept north and captured the city of Jerusalem in 637. Turning east, the Muslims overran central Asia. By 712, they had captured the ancient city of Samarkand, on the main trade route to China.

At the same time, other Muslim armies conquered Egypt and northern Africa. In 711, the Muslims crossed the Straits of Gibraltar and attacked Spain. Now, all of Europe was threatened. Would Muslim forces take over the whole world? Finally, in 732, Christian armies stopped the Muslims' advance by defeating them just south of Paris, France.

Even though the Muslim forces were unable to overtake most of western Europe, they had gained control over a very large part of the world. Just 100

This mosque was built in Córdoba, Spain after the city was conquered by the Muslims.

years after Muhammad's death, his followers ruled a vast empire that stretched one-quarter of the way around the globe—from the Atlantic Ocean in the west to India in the east.

The Search for Knowledge

According to Islamic beliefs, Muslims have a duty to seek knowledge wherever they go. As Muslim soldiers conquered new lands, they collected ancient documents, so they could learn about the history, traditions, and teachings of other cultures. They were especially interested in the ideas of ancient scientists.

The Muslims learned about medicine and mathematics from ancient Greek and Egyptian documents. The ancient Greeks, Persians, and the people of India had accumulated a great deal of information about the stars and planets. The Muslims gathered knowledge about engineering from Egypt and Mesopotamia—an ancient civilization that emerged along the Tigris and Euphrates rivers. (The Mesopotamian Empire included land that is now part of Turkey, Syria, Iraq, and Iran.) From India came the knowledge of numbers, including the use of the zero to indicate "nothing" or "none." All this learning was preserved in Muslim libraries and educational centers.

chapter 2

A New View of Numbers

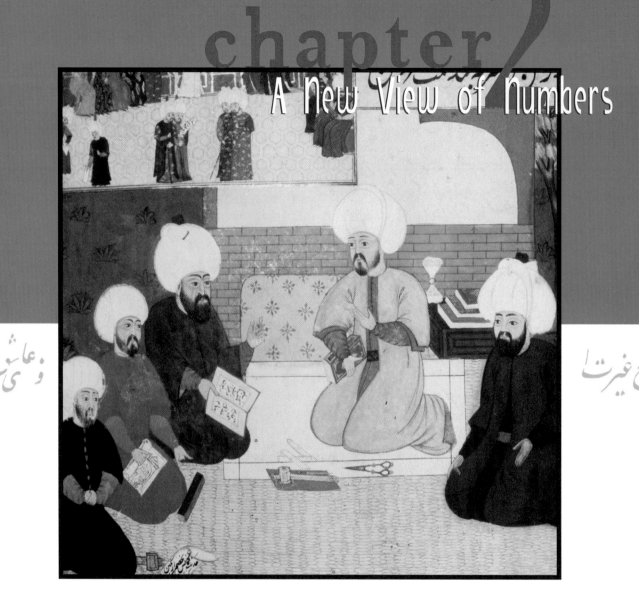

كو تع غيرت ا

و عاشق

Muslims recognized the benefits of
the Arabic system of numbers and
began using it.

Numeric Symbols

ARABIC	GREEK	ROMAN
1	A	I
2	B	II
3	Γ	III
4	Δ	IV
5	E	V
6	F	VI
7	Z	VII
8	H	VIII
9	Θ	IX
10	I	X
20	K	XX
30	Λ	XXX
40	M	XL
50	N	L
60	Ξ	LX
70	O	LXX
80	Π	LXXX
90	Q	XC
100	P	C

When the Muslim armies reached Mesopotamia in the 600s, they found mathematicians using numbers that looked strange and different. Today we call these numbers "Arabic numerals." The system had been invented in India, but it was the Muslims in Arabia who recognized its usefulness. Arabic numerals were soon used throughout the Islamic world, and eventually spread to western Europe.

At that time, people in western Europe used many different numerical systems. The Greeks, who had influenced people in the area surrounding the Mediterranean Sea, used letters of their alphabet to stand for numbers. The Romans, who had conquered most of Europe as well as parts of Africa and Asia, also used a system based on letters.

The system developed in India was much simpler than those used by the Greeks and Romans. Using just nine different symbols, plus the zero, it was possible to write any number—no matter how big it might be.

When the symbol "1" appears alone, it always means 1 unit. When the symbol "1" is followed by one other number symbol, such as 5, it represents tens. In the number 15, 1 stands for tens and 5 stands for units. The symbol "1" followed by two other symbols stands for hundreds. For example, in the number 132, the 1 stands for hundreds, the 3 stands for tens, and the 2 stands for units.

According to this system, moving a number to the left increases its value by ten times—10 is ten times greater than 1; 100 is ten times greater than 10; and 1,000 is ten times greater than 100. This numerical system should seem familiar to you because everyone in the world uses it today.

A few Western mathematicians knew about Arabic numerals in the 600s. However, the system was not accepted throughout the Islamic world until the 800s, when it was praised by Al-Khwarizmi, one of the greatest Muslim mathematicians.

How Higher Math Developed

In his writings, Al-Khwarizmi explained the principles of a form of math he called "al-jabr." Today, we call this type of math *algebra* and most students learn about it in high school. Although algebra was first used by the Greeks and Egyptians, it was refined by Al-Khwarizmi.

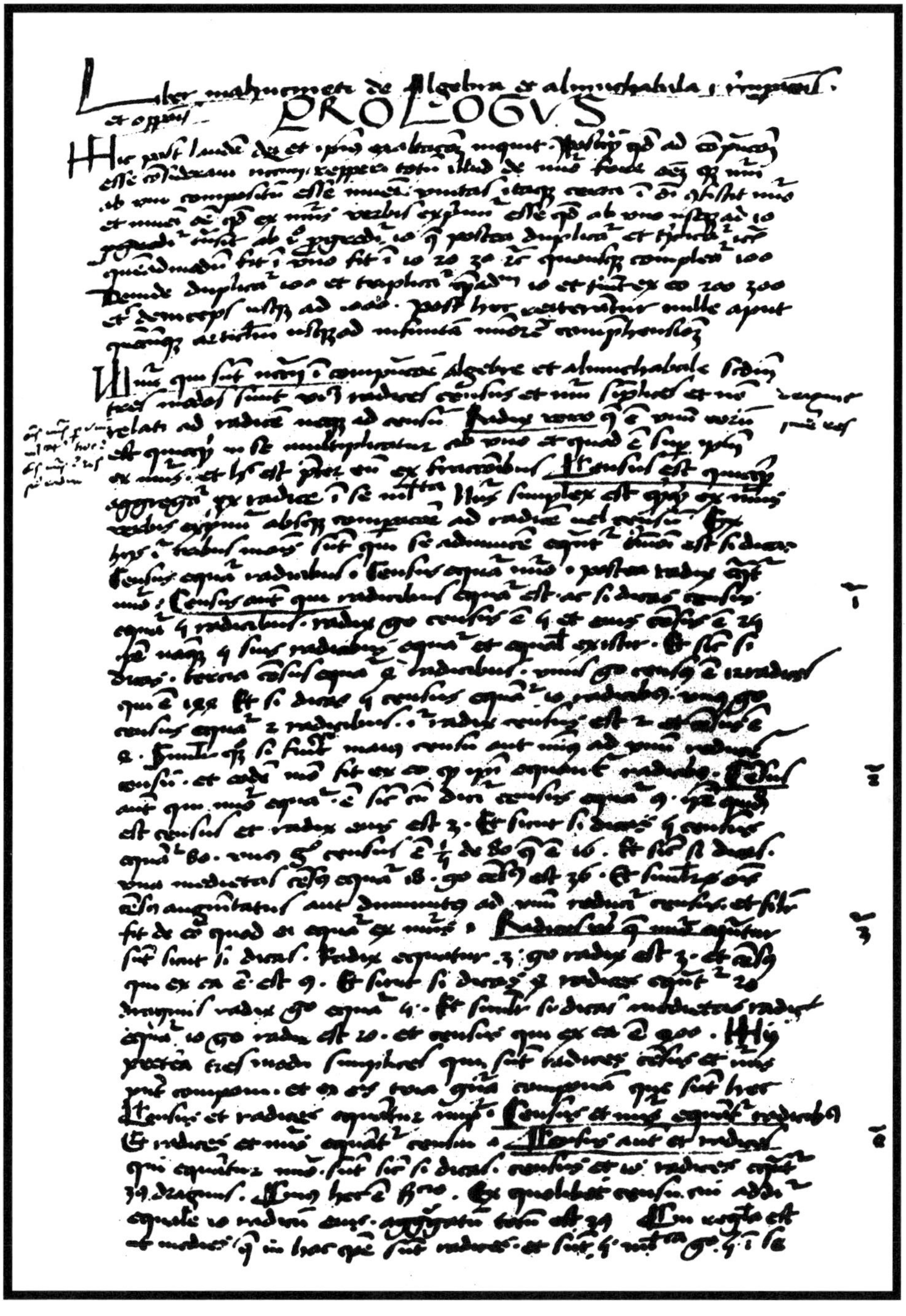

The first page of Al-Khwarizmi's book about algebra

In algebra, problems are often written in the form of *equations,* which include letters of the alphabet to represent the unknown numbers. The goal of algebra is to figure out what number the letter stands for. For example, in the equation $3 \times x = 12$, the goal is to find out what number x stands for. In this case, x stands for the number 4 because $3 \times 4 = 12$.

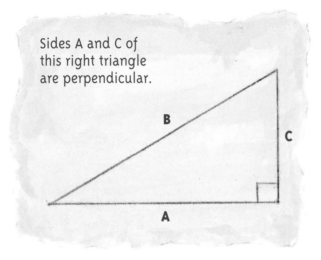

Sides A and C of this right triangle are perpendicular.

Islamic mathematicians also found new ways to calculate the distance to an object that was very far away. This type of math, which is called *trigonometry,* is used by surveyors and astronomers. Islamic mathematicians worked out detailed tables that can be used to determine the relationship between the sides of any right triangle—a type of triangle that always has two *perpendicular* sides.

Here's an example. Let's say that a group of surveyors wants to figure out how much it will cost to build a bridge across a swift-flowing river. How can they do this? They can use objects to mark the points of an imaginary triangle and then use trigonometry to *estimate* the width of the river.

First, they choose an object, such as a rock, close to the opposite shore. Then they place a stick in the ground directly across from the rock. Next, they place a second stick in the ground farther downstream. The surveyors then measure the distance between the two sticks and

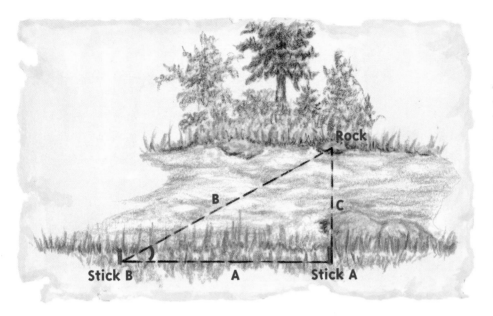

Muslim surveyors could find the distance across a river by creating an imaginary right triangle. They measured the length of side A, determined the size of angles AB and BC, and then plugged the values into a mathematical formula.

measure the angle between each stick and the rock across the river. These measurements give them all the information they need to calculate the width of the river. Using the trigonometry tables provided by the Muslim mathematicians, the surveyors can find the length of the side of the triangle that corresponds to the river's width.

Mission: Measure the Earth

People have always been curious about the size and shape of our planet. Careful observers living in the earliest civilizations thought the world was round. When they looked at Earth's shadow on the moon during an eclipse, they saw that it was curved. Only a *sphere,* an object shaped like a ball, could create that type of shadow. Other observers noticed that as ships approached the shore, their tall sails came into view before the ships' hulls. This suggested that the ship was sailing on a curved sea. Despite this evidence, up to the 1400s, many people believed the world was flat.

About 2,300 years ago, a Greek mathematician named Eratosthenes determined the angle to the sun from two different places along the Nile River. He then measured the distance between these two points. From these measurements, Eratosthenes concluded that the distance around Earth was about 28,000 to 29,000 miles (45,000 to 47,000 km). His estimate was extremely close to the value that scientists accept today—24,860 miles (40,008 km).

Muslim scholars found and preserved Eratosthenes's manuscripts and other similar documents. In 830, a Muslim ruler built a huge center of learning called the House of Wisdom in Baghdad, the capital of what is now Iraq. When the House of Wisdom was completed, the ruler asked the scholars who worked there to measure the Earth's *circumference.*

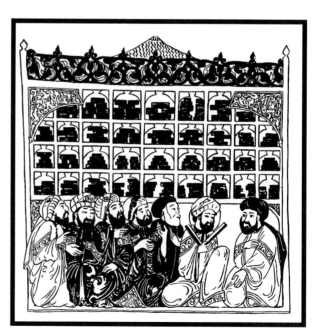

Following the procedures used by Eratosthenes and another Greek *astronomer* named Posidonius of Apamea, the mathematicians at the House of Wisdom measured the distance between two cities and found the angle of the sun from each of them. Their

Scholars meeting at the House of Wisdom

The Muslims collected ancient documents, such as this Egyptian scroll that describes how the pyramids were built.

methods were correct, but their measurements were not. As a result, they estimated that the distance around Earth was 20,400 miles (32,830 km).

Muslim scholars continued to search through the ancient manuscripts coming into Baghdad and other major Islamic centers of learning. From these they learned more and more about ancient scientific views of the world and the heavens.

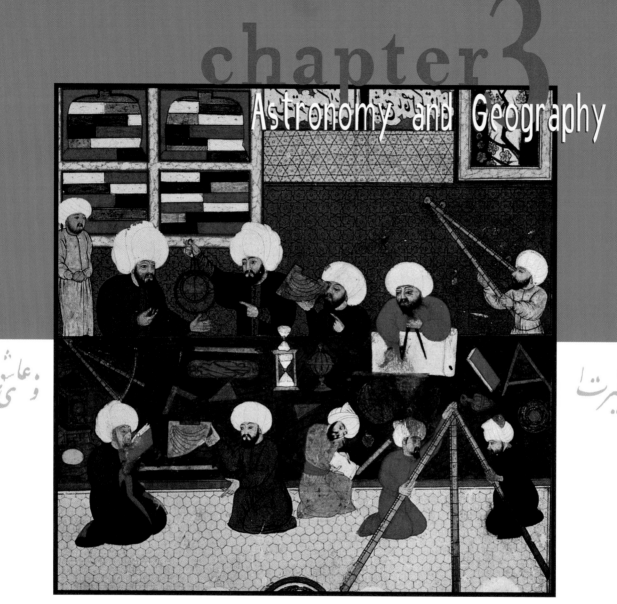

This representation of Islamic astronomers is part of a 500-year-old painting.

Many of the ancient manuscripts that Arab traders brought back from foreign lands dealt with *astronomy,* the study of the stars and planets. These documents included extensive charts created by the ancient stargazers of Greece, Persia, and India, showing the apparent movements of heavenly bodies across the night skies. The ancient Greeks had even learned to predict eclipses.

The Muslims gathered all this material together and published it, so that it was available to astronomers and *astrologers.* The astrologers thought they could use this information to foretell events in people's lives. To do this, they plotted a chart showing the positions of stars and planets at the time of a person's birth, especially those rising on the horizon.

An Islamic astrologer reading the position of the stars

Our Solar System

Greek astronomers living about 2,300 years ago believed that Earth revolved around the sun. Even though they were correct, this idea was lost for many centuries. About 1,800 years ago, a respected Greek astronomer and mapmaker named Claudius Ptolemaeus (also known as Ptolemy) lived in Alexandria, Egypt. Ptolemy convinced the leading scholars of his time that our planet—Earth—is at the center of the universe.

Ptolemy believed that the sun and planets orbited Earth. An artist created this painting based on Ptolemy's view of the universe.

According to the *Ptolemaic system*, the sun, moon, and planets traveled around Earth in perfect circles. Ptolemy drew up detailed charts to show each planet's movements. He used these charts to predict when each planet would rise and set on Earth's horizon and when each would reach its *zenith*, its highest position in the sky.

The Greeks who lived after Ptolemy, the Muslims, and most Europeans accepted Ptolemy's theory, even though it did not always accurately predict the movement of the planets. To explain the difference between his theory and what astronomers observed, Ptolemy—and scholars who came after him—developed increasingly complicated sub-theories. Finally, in 1543, a Polish astronomer named Nicolaus Copernicus challenged Ptolemy's ideas.

Copernicus was bold enough to propose a model of the solar system that had the sun, not Earth, at the center. He believed that all the planets, including Earth, rotate around the sun and that the moon rotates around Earth. Copernicus's ideas were not accepted until many years later.

Copernicus proposed that the sun was at the center of our solar system. sun. An artist created this painting based on Copernicu's ideas.

In the 1600s, Danish astronomer Tycho Brahe carefully recorded the planets' positions over tyhe course of several years. Using this information and his knowledge of mathematics, Johannes Kepler developed a way of accurately predicting how the planets would move in the future.In order for his calculations to work, Kepler had to assume that the sun—not Earth—was at the center of the solar system.

Galileo's first
telescope

At about the same time, an Italian astronomer and physicist named Galileo Galilei began to carefully study the planets with a new device—the telescope. Galileo's observations convinced him that Copernicus had been right. Soon other scientists began to agree with the idea that the sun is at the center of the solar system.

An astrolabe

The Astrolabe

One of the first instruments ever used to measure the *altitude* of a star or planet above the horizon is called an *astrolabe*. It was invented at least 2,100 years ago by the Greeks. The word "astrolabe" comes from two Greek words—*astro*, which means "star" and *labio*, which means "finder."

The astrolabe consists of two flat circular discs. One is a star map that shows the positions of the brightest stars in the sky as well as the paths of the sun and the planets. The second disc shows the zenith, the horizon, and the lines of altitude for a specific latitude. Both discs are held in a case that has a scale of the hours engraved on the rim.

By using an astrolabe to view the North Star, Muslim mapmakers and sailors could determined their *latitude*, or horizontal position on Earth. By viewing the sun and other stars with the astrolabe, they could determine the time.

Build Your Own Astrolabe

You can build a simple astrolabe. You will need a square piece of cardboard about 6 inches (15 cm) on each side, a protractor, a drinking straw, masking tape, a marking pen, a needle, a piece of string, and a washer.

1. Using the protractor, draw lines at ten degree intervals. Be sure the $0°$ and $90°$ lines are parallel to the edges of the cardboard.

2. Tape a drinking straw to the edge of the cardboard square, so that it is parallel to the $90°$ line.

3. Using the needle, make a tiny hole at the point where all the degree lines meet.

4. Next, thread a piece of string through the hole. Knot the end of the string on the back side of the cardboard several times so that the knot does not slip through the hole.

5. Finally, tie a metal washer to the other end of the string, so that the string is under tension. When you hold the astrolabe with the $90°$ line perfectly straight, the string should lie along the $0°$ line.

When you look at a star through the straw, the string will mark the altitude of the star in degrees. If you view the North Star, your altitude reading will tell you your latitude. *Do not try to measure the sun's altitude with your astrolabe. Looking directly at the sun can damage your eyes.*

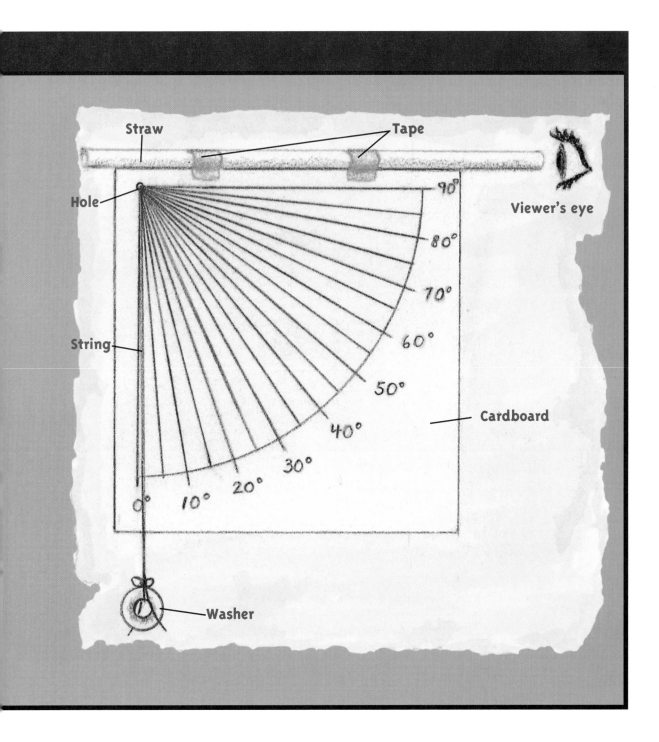

Straw

Tape

Hole

Viewer's eye

String

Cardboard

90°
80°
70°
60°
50°
40°
30°
20°
10°
0°

Washer

Watching the Sun

Since the days of the early Greeks, stargazers have carefully watched the sun's apparent path across the sky.* These ancient astronomers noticed that the sun crosses the equator twice each year—once in March and once in September. On the days when the sun crosses the equator, there are exactly 12 hours of daylight and exactly 12 hours of darkness. These crossings are called *equinoxes* because equi- means "equal" and -nox is related to the word "nocturnal," which means "night." The spring equinox usually occurs on March 21, and the fall equinox usually occurs on September 23.

Greek astronomer Hipparchus looking at a star-filled sky

Greek astronomers kept careful records of the sun's position during each equinox. By the year 100, they noticed that the sun does not always pass over the same point along the equator. Eventually, scientists realized that the gravitational

---

* Scientists refer to the path as "apparent" because the sun does not really cross the sky. It only seems that way to viewers on Earth. In reality, the sun is stationary and the Earth rotates around it.

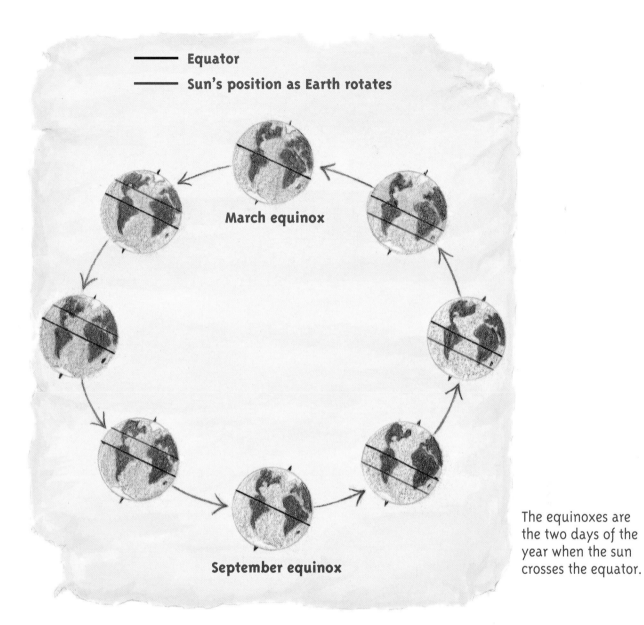

Equator
Sun's position as Earth rotates

March equinox

September equinox

The equinoxes are the two days of the year when the sun crosses the equator.

pull of the moon and sun causes Earth to wobble slightly, like a top that is spinning on a table. To meticulous Greek observers, this wobbling made it seem like the sun's path was drifting farther to the west each year.

Although neither the Greeks nor the Muslims were able to imagine why the sun's path seemed to change, the Muslims accurately measured this change. They found that each equinox occurred about 1.5 percent of a degree to the west of the previous one. This change is hardly noticeable, yet the ancient Greeks were observant enough to notice it and the ancient Muslims had the mathematical knowledge to calculate it.

An Accurate Calendar

In their search for knowledge, the Muslims collected documents that charted the movement of stars, planets, and the moon over hundreds of years. They used all this information to create extremely accurate calendars.

Calendars were as important in ancient Islam as they are to us today. Calendars helped farmers know when to plant and harvest crops. They were also important to travelers and traders who needed to know when they could safely cross snow-covered mountains and blazing deserts.

Omar Khayyam, a Persian astronomer and poet, was a

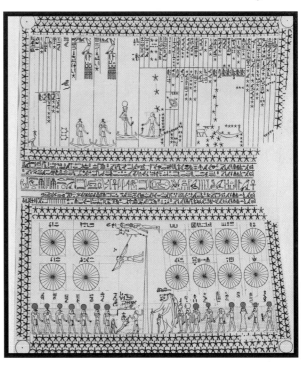

This painting on the ceiling of a tomb includes information about the movement of the stars and planets.

Omar Khayyam
working on his
calendar.

Muslim who lived from 1048 to 1131. While in charge of an observatory in Persia, Khayyam devised a new calendar. His calendar was off by only 1 day in 5,000 years. That's more accurate than the calendar used today! Unfortunately, Omar Khayyam's calendar was never widely accepted because people did not want to give up the older, more familiar ones. They didn't seem to care that Khayyam's calendar was much more reliable.

Mapping Earth

As the Muslim armies conquered new lands, they were followed by astronomers and mapmakers who studied the skies and terrain of these areas. These scientists wanted to know whether the stars looked different in different parts of the world and why some areas received more rainfall than others. The Muslims also calculated the height of mountains and other land formations. All of these observations and measurements helped them design more accurate maps.

These maps listed the *longitude* of a designated place in degrees east or west. (On today's maps, all longitude is measured in degrees east or west of the *prime meridian,* which passes through Greenwich, England.) Today, geographers use lines of

A group of scientists and mapmakers studying areas recently conquered by Muslim armies

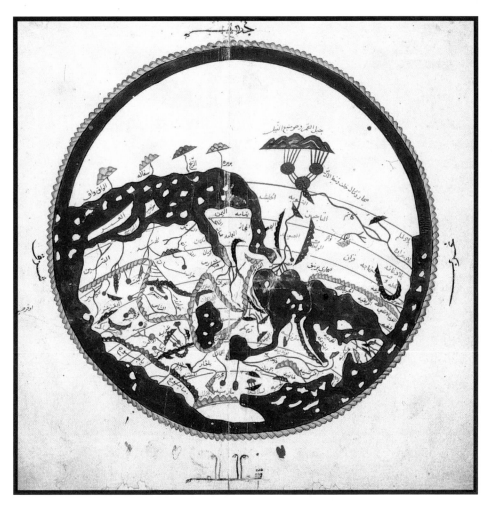

An early Islamic
map of the world

latitude to indicate a site's horizontal position on Earth. Muslim map-makers accomplished this by listing the length of daylight in a specific place on the *summer solstice,* which usually occurs on June 22. If the length of time between sunrise and sunset on that day was exactly the same in a city in Spain and a town in central Asia, the mapmakers knew the two places were the same distance north of the equator.

A Muslim physician examining a
patient

While Muslim astronomers searched the heavens to discover the secrets of the universe, other scientists wondered why people got sick and how they could be cured. They looked within the human body for the answers to their questions. The medical tradition of Islam goes back to the earliest days of Muslim rule.

Islamic medicine was based on information gathered from the Greeks, the Persians, and the people of India. Most of the ancient books and documents collected by the Muslims included folklore about herbs and drugs. As time passed, Muslim doctors added information based on their own experiences.

Muslim doctors knew how to use sedatives—drugs that help people relax or sleep. They also used hashish, a drug made from the same plant as marijuana, as a painkiller after surgery. By the year 1000, a Muslim doctor named Al-Zahrawi began using *antiseptics* to clean wounds. The importance of cleaning wounds was not routinely recognized by Western doctors until the 1800s.

Muslim physicians studied medical texts written by ancient Egyptians, Greeks, and Romans.

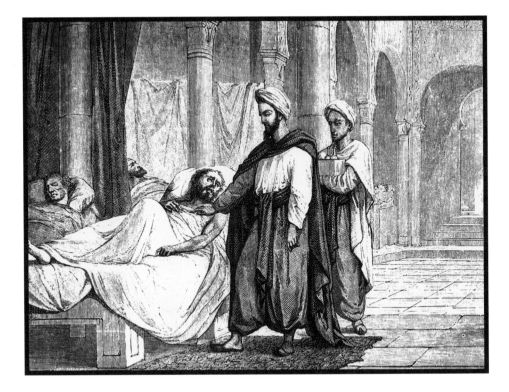

The Islamic healer Al-Zahrawi developed a number of important medical techniques.

Al-Zahrawi also used *sutures* made from animal intestines and silk to stitch surgical wounds. He even designed a number of surgical instruments, including knives, scalpels, probes, and hooks.

Muslim Hospitals

In 707, just 75 years after the death of Muhammad, Muslim leaders founded a hospital in Damascus, in what is now Syria. The hospital, which was staffed with doctors paid by the government, provided a full range of free medical services. This hospital became the model for medical centers throughout the Islamic world.

Islamic medical centers were like today's teaching hospitals. They provided medical care to people with all sorts of injuries and diseases and gave young doctors an opportunity to learn about the causes of—and treatments for—various medical conditions.

After a period of training, all doctors were required to pass a series of examinations. In many cities, druggists and barbers, who often bled people as a medical treatment, were also required to follow certain regulations.

Islamic hospitals, which treated both men and women, received all or most of their funding from the government. In the 1000s, medical care was extended to people living in rural areas, prisons, and inner-city areas. In most other parts of the world, quality medical care was available only to royalty and rich landowners.

In many parts of the Islamic world, druggists were required to pass a medical test before they could sell herbal remedies.

The Heart and Lungs

One of the greatest breakthroughs in medical knowledge came in the 1200s. A Muslim doctor named Ibn an-Nafis realized that blood circulates throughout the body—a finding that contradicted ancient medical beliefs. Around the year 100, a Roman physician named Galen had written that blood is manufactured in the liver as needed by the body and flows back and forth between the left and right sides of the heart.

Ibn an-Nafis wrote that the right side of the heart pumps blood to the lungs, where it is purified. The blood then returns to the left side of the heart, and is pumped through the arteries that carry the blood to the rest

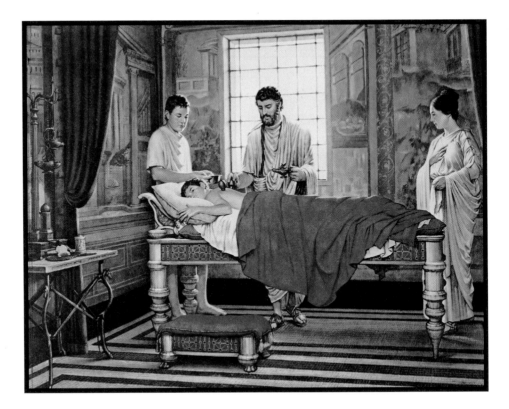

Galen treating a patient

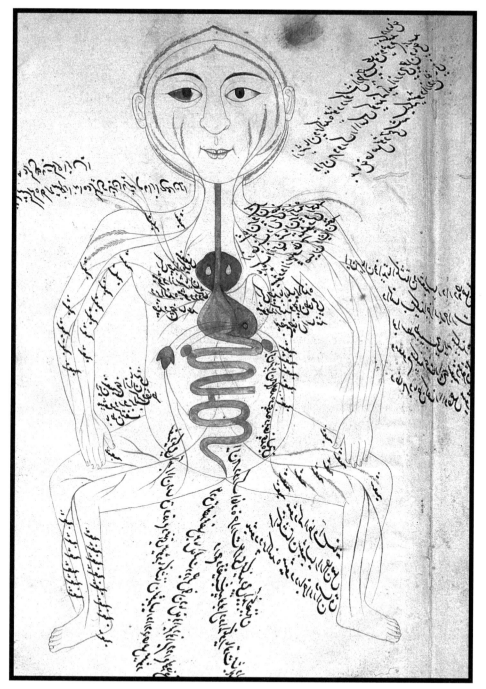

This drawing of a human's internal organs first appeared in an Islamic text called *The Anatomy of the Human Body*.

of the body. Next, the blood passes through the veins and returns to the right side of the heart where the process starts all over again. This is basically the way that modern medicine describes the circulatory system.

Ibn an-Nafis was not sure how blood gets from the arteries to the veins. That mystery was solved by a Muslim doctor named Ibn al-Quff, who lived from 1233 to 1286. Because he worked in a hospital at the time of the Crusades, he treated many Muslim soldiers. These soldiers were wounded fighting Christian armies who wanted to recapture Jerusalem and other holy places.

Ibn al-Quff wrote that tiny capillaries allowed the blood to flow from the arteries to the veins. He also described the function of the *cardial valves* in the veins and heart chambers. Because these valves open in only one direction, they ensure that all blood in the circulatory system flows in the same direction.

A Muslim physician treating a wounded soldier

Ibn Sina writing the text for one of his books

The Healing Process

Other Muslim doctors made valuable discoveries and wrote extensively about them. A doctor named Al-Razi, who lived from about 865 to 925, wrote close to 180 documents and books, including a 20-volume series that discussed every branch of medicine. Another smaller volume, called *Treatise on Smallpox and Measles,* was the first accurate study of infectious disease to become available in the West.

Ibn Sina, one of the greatest Muslim doctors, lived about 100 years later. He spent most of his life learning the secrets of healing. When he was only 20 years old, he was known as the most learned man of his time. He studied the patients who came to the free clinics he established.

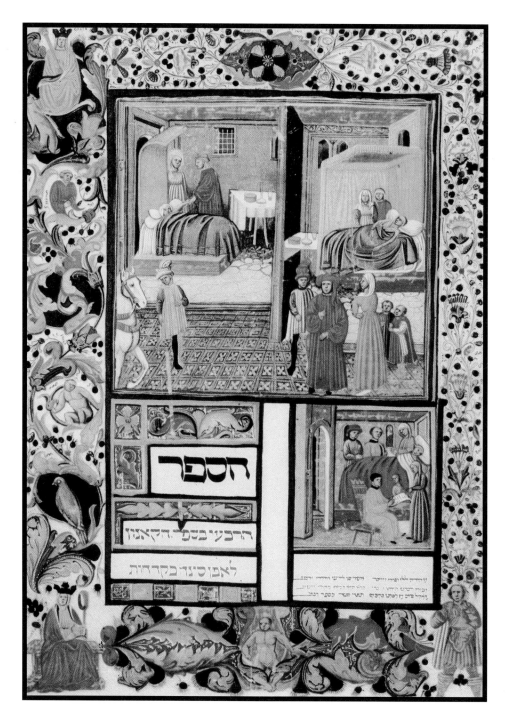

A page from Ibn
Sina's book *The
Canon of Medicine*

42

Ibn Sina believed that most health problems occur because people do things that block their bodies' natural healing mechanisms. For example, when someone uses a sore arm instead of resting it, the pain gets worse because the body cannot heal itself. He thought that sleep was very important for sick people because it gave their bodies' natural healing mechanisms a chance to work. According to Ibn Sina, if people with ordinary colds did not take proper care of themselves, they might develop pneumonia or other serious complications.

Ibn Sina kept careful notes and wrote many books to share his ideas with other physicians. In all, he wrote close to 270 different documents and books on medicine and philosophy. One of Ibn Sina's best-known works is a multi-volume series called *The Canon of Medicine*. It contains enough information to fill more than 5,000 pages of a modern book. In *The Canon of Medicine,* Ibn Sina summarized the history and traditions of medical practice accumulated over more than 1,000 years.

chapter 5

Unraveling the Mysteries of the Universe

Ibn al-Haytham explaining how
the reflection of light makes vision
possible

Understanding How We See

For centuries, scientists and philosophers wondered about the secrets behind human vision. According to a theory developed by Greek philosophers who lived about 2,300 years ago, the body sends out a special ray that makes sight possible. Because Ptolemy—the Greek scholar you learned about in Chapter 3—agreed with this idea, most people accepted it. Galen—the Roman physician mentioned in Chapter 4—believed that sight has something to do with the lens of the eye. He suspected that a nerve connected the eye to the brain. Muslims weren't sure which theory to believe so they began to develop their own ideas about human vision.

Ibn al-Haytham, a Muslim scientist who lived around 1000, studied how light travels through *transparent* materials, such as glass and water. Based on his observations, Ibn al-Haytham suggested that light is emitted by all radiant sources and travels in a straight line. In addition, when beams of light

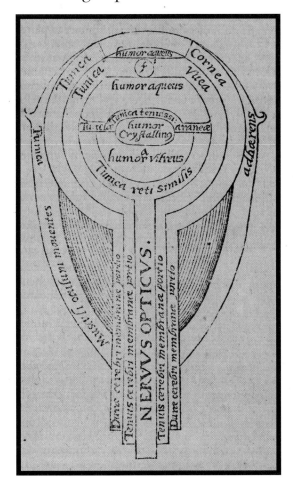

Ibn al-Haytham's diagram of the eye with the parts labeled in Latin

fall on an object, the light is reflected back to the eye. This reflected light sends signals to the brain, making sight possible. Ibn al-Haytham's ideas mark the beginning of our modern knowledge of light and vision.

Ibn al-Haytham was the first scientist to realize that light travels through air and water at different speeds. He discovered this difference causes the part of the drinking straw below the water's surface to be thrown slightly out of line with the portion above the water's surface.

Refraction of Light

Ibn al-Haytham was also able to explain a phenomenon that had puzzled ancient thinkers for centuries. You can see this interesting effect for yourself.

1. Fill a clear drinking glass with water or ginger ale.
2. Put a drinking straw in the glass and view the drinking straw from above and from the side.

Does the drinking straw look the same from above as it does from the side? It shouldn't. From overhead, the drinking straw should look the same as it did before you put it in the glass. From the side, however, the drinking straw will seem to be broken. When a beam of light passes through a transparent material, such as water, it slows down and bends. This bending, which is called *refraction,* makes the drinking straw look like it is broken.

Muslim scientists understood how light was reflected by raindrops to create a rainbow.

Mysteries of the Rainbow

Ancient thinkers did not know how a combination of sunlight and rain could produce a rainbow. Nor could they explain why a rainbow's colors always appear in the same order—red, orange, yellow, green, blue, and violet. Ibn al-Haytham also wrestled unsuccessfully with these questions.

It was not until the 1300s that Muslim scientists conducted experiments that helped them understand how rainbows form. First, they made a small hole in a piece of material. Then they placed the material in front of a window. When they allowed sunlight to pass through the hole and then through a glass sphere filled with water, the sunlight was *dispersed* and reflected. As a result, the sunlight was separated into all the colors of the rainbow.

The scientists realized that the glass sphere in their lab was doing what falling raindrops do. As sunlight passes through raindrops, it is separated and forms a colorful rainbow in the sky.

Secrets of Alchemy

Other scientists were more intrigued by information gathered from ancient China and India. These documents contained long lists of formulas and chemical recipes developed over several centuries by alchemists. These texts are actually the earliest traces of what we now call chemistry.

Alchemy seems to have originated in China and spread first to India and then to Persia, Egypt, and Greece. Early alchemists were searching for what they called an *elixir of life*. They believed that by mixing just the right combination of materials, they could create a potent magical potion that would allow them to live forever.

Other alchemists looked for ways to change common metals—such as lead, copper, arsenic, iron, and zinc—into gold. When they mixed a tiny bit of arsenic with copper, the result was a beautiful golden-colored metal. If they added a little more arsenic to the mixture, the final

Many alchemists hoped to create gold from inexpensive materials.

Alchemists used symbols such as dragons to represent chemical processes.

product was a shiny, silver-like substance. Results such as these encouraged the alchemists to keep looking for a way to create pure gold out of cheaper metals.

The substances that alchemists chose often reacted with each other and formed completely new substances. Although they were never able to create gold, they did produce a number of materials with useful properties. For example, by combining copper and zinc carbonate, they created brass. If they mixed copper and tin, the result was bronze. Because

Muslim alchemists developed the technique for making steel from iron.

brass and bronze are the same color as gold, these discoveries caused a great deal of excitement.

Muslim alchemists made a very important discovery. The found a way to make iron, one of the most common materials in the ground, very hard. After repeatedly hammering and heating the iron in a certain way, they dunked it in water or oil to cool it quickly. What they ended up with was steel. Because steel is very strong, they began using it to make weapons and farm tools. Today steel girders support the world's tallest skyscrapers.

Although some alchemists were really just trying to cheat kings and other rich people out of their money, many sincerely believed that it was possible to transform cheaper metals into gold. They thought they were very close to finding just the right chemical recipe. And, even though alchemists never did find a way to produce gold, they learned a lot about how chemicals react with one another.

chapter 6

Scientific Accomplishments of Islam

This page from *The Creation and Curiosities of Existence* discusses the zodiac constellations Pisces and Aquarius.

52

The early Muslims made great strides in science. Because they carefully collected, preserved, and studied knowledge accumulated by the world's ancient civilizations, they quickly developed a basic understanding of math, astronomy, medicine, alchemy, the properties of light, and navigation. The Muslims then conducted their own experiments and learned even more about the world around them.

For more than 500 years, the Muslims leaders ruled a vast empire and Muslim scholars devoted most of their time to science. Eventually, however, the Islamic world began to have trouble maintaining its power. Some Muslims began to question their faith. This led to internal struggles. At the same time, the strength of the Islamic world was being threatened by invasions from the east and west.

In 1099, Christian Crusaders from Europe captured Jerusalem. It took the Muslims 100 years to regain control of the city. The

European crusaders fighting for control of Jerusalem

Crusaders also regained control of Córdoba, Spain. This was a major victory because Córdoba was a wealthy city with a great mosque and a library that held close to 500,000 books.

Around 1100, warriors also began attacking the eastern borders of the Islamic world. Armies of Mongolians captured and burned Baghdad in the 1200s. The city was rebuilt, but fell to the Mongolians again in 1400.

During these battles, records of some of Islam's great medical discoveries, such as the use of antiseptics and anesthesia, were lost. Luckily, a great deal of medical knowledge was preserved. Ibn Sina's great *Canon of Medicine* was translated into Latin in the 1100s and became the basic text used in European medical schools. The information in Al-Razi's 20-volume work on medicine and his small book on smallpox and measles were also used to teach medical students in Europe.

European scholars also benefited from the Islamic knowledge of light. They used the principles of refraction to develop lenses for telescopes and microscopes.

Uncovering Mistakes Made by Muslim Scientists

Muslim scientists made many contributions to modern science, but they also made some mistakes. As you learned in Chapter 2, Muslim astronomers measured the Earth's circumference incorrectly. For centuries afterward, scientists all over the world accepted their calculations.

When Christopher Columbus planned his historic voyage in 1492, he used the Islamic figures to estimate how long it would take him to reach the East Indies. If Columbus had known the actual distance to Asia, he might never have attempted the trip.

Columbus's ships—the *Nina,* the *Pinta,* and the *Santa Maria*—landed in the West Indies in 1492.

Muslim scientists also made the mistake of accepting Ptolemy's view of the solar system. As you learned in Chapter 3, Ptolemy believed that Earth was at the center of the solar system. Although Muslims' observations of the stars and planets began to cast doubt on this idea, the Muslims never understood the true relationship between the sun and Earth.

Roots of the Scientific Method

Some Muslim scientists based their work on the ideas of a Greek philosopher named Plato who lived about 2,300 years ago. Plato believed that people should look within themselves for the important things in life, such as love and beauty.

This detail from a fresco painted by Raphael shows Plato (left) and Aristotle (right).

In this symbolic painting, Aristotle is showing three Muslim scientists how to use an astrolabe.

Other scientists preferred another Greek philosopher's views of the world. Aristotle, who was originally Plato's pupil, believed that people should search for knowledge outside themselves. Aristotle encouraged people to study the world around them. He thought humans could discover truths about nature only through experience and experimentation.

For many centuries, Muslim scientists were pulled back and forth between the Platonic and the Aristotelian approaches to learning. As time passed, however, Aristotle's way of thinking began to have more influence over the way Muslim's practiced science. The Muslim decision to adopt Aristotle's way of investigating the world had profound affects on modern science.

Today, scientists see themselves as careful, unbiased observers of the world and everything in it. To test their ideas, modern researchers use an approach called the *scientific method*. First, they clearly state the purpose of their investigation. This includes proposing a *hypothesis,* a statement that tells what they hope to learn from the experiment. Next, the scientists conduct a series of experiments and record the results. Finally, they reach a conclusion based on the data they have collected.

By following this process, scientists can get all the information they need to either accept or reject their original hypothesis. The scientific method is based on Aristotle's view of studying and understanding the world.

A Bridge Between Ancient Science and Modern Science

It was great Muslim thinkers like Al-Khwarizmi, Ibn Sina, and Ibn al-Haytham who took the collective knowledge of the ancient civilizations and used it to develop entirely new ideas and theories.

Thus, Islamic science provided a bridge between the scientific discoveries of the world's most ancient cultures and modern knowledge of and approach to science. Because the Muslims preserved ancient texts, we have access to thousands of years of scientific thought. When Europeans rediscovered this wealth of knowledge, it spurred the new interest in science and scientific discovery that characterized the Renaissance. That same scientific spirit has been carried across time and continues to inspire us today.

GLOSSARY

alchemy—an ancient quest for knowledge through magical means, including a search for ways to extend life and turn common metals into gold.

algebra—a branch of mathematics in which unknown numbers are represented by letters of the alphabet. The value of the unknowns is determined by manipulating the equations.

altitude—the angular distance above the horizon.

antiseptic—a substance that prevents or slows down the growth of germs.

astrolabe—an instrument used to determine the angles of the sun, stars, or planets above the horizon.

astrologer—a person who studies the stars in order to foretell future events.

astronomer—a scientist who studies stars and planets.

astronomy—the scientific study of the stars and planets.

cardial valves—valves in the circulatory system that open only one way, keeping the blood flowing in the same direction at all times.

circumference—the distance around Earth at its widest part.

disperse—to break up or spread.

elixir of life—a mythical magic potion sought by alchemists to extend life or increase youthfulness.

equation—a mathematical term that says two expressions are equal.

equinox—the two times of the year (in March and September) when the sun is over the equator and day and night are exactly equal in length.

estimate—to judge; to appraise.

hypothesis—a statement that scientists hope to prove or disprove with an experiment.

Islam—the religion based on the teachings of Muhammad.

latitude—imaginary lines encircling Earth from east to west. The equator is one line of latitude.

longitude—imaginary lines encircling Earth and passing through the North and South Poles.

Muslim—a person who follows the faith of Islam.

perpendicular—meeting at a right angle.

prime meridian—the line of longitude that passes through Greenwich, England.

Ptolemaic system—the system of thought that placed Earth at the center of the universe. It is named after Ptolemy, a Greek mathematician and astronomer who lived in Alexandria, Egypt around the year 100.

refraction—an apparent change in position of an object (such as a drinking straw in water) caused by light traveling at different speeds in two different mediums, such as air and water.

scientific method—a system of investigation.

sphere—an object shaped like a ball. Earth is a sphere.

summer solstice—the time of year when the sun crosses directly over the Tropic of Cancer. It marks the longest day of the year in the Northern Hemisphere and the shortest day of the year in the Southern Hemisphere.

sutures—fibers used to sew parts of a living body.

transparent—can be seen through. When you look through a transparent object, such as glass, or a transparent fluid, such as water, objects on the other side look the same as if there was nothing between you and the object.

trigonometry—the branch of mathematics dealing with angles and triangles.

zenith—a star or planet's highest position in the sky.

RESOURCES

Books

Al-Hassan, Ahmad Y., and Donald R. Hill. *Islamic Technology: An Illustrated History.* Cambridge: Cambridge University Press, 1992.

Hill, Donald R. *Islamic Science and Engineering.* Chicago: Kazi Publications, Inc., 1995.

Huff, Toby E. *The Rise of Early Modern Science: Islam, China, and the West.* Cambridge: Cambridge University Press, 1993.

Lippman, Thomas W. *Understanding Islam: An Introduction to the Muslim World.* New York: NAL Dutton, 1995.

Nasr, Seyyed H. *Islamic Science: An Illustrated Study.* Chicago: Kazi Publications, Inc., 1995.

Internet Site

Due to the changeable nature of the Internet, sites appear and disappear very quickly. The following resources offered useful information on the ancient world at the time of publication.

Exploring Ancient World Culture includes maps, timelines, essays, and images that describe ancient civilizations in India, China, Greece, and the Near East. It can be reached at **http://eawc.evansville.edu/index.htm.**

INDEX

ABOUT THE AUTHOR

George Beshore has written about scientific and environmental subjects for newspapers, magazines, and the federal government for more than 40 years. He has written one other book for the Science of the Past series. Mr. Beshore lives in Alexandria, Virginia, with his wife, Margaret.